HAL•LEONARD

INSTRUMENTAL PLAY-ALONG

AUDIO ACCESS INCLUDED

PLAYBACK+
Speed • Pitch • Balance • Loop

A NEW MUSICAL
Wicked

D0613645

To access audio visit:
www.halleonard.com/mylibrary

Enter Code
4019-1848-4537-8325

ISBN: 978-1-4234-4975-1

HAL•LEONARD® CORPORATION

7777 W. BLUEMOUND RD. P.O. BOX 13819 MILWAUKEE, WI 53213

Visit Hal Leonard Online at
www.halleonard.com

AS LONG AS YOU'RE MINE

Music and Lyrics by
STEPHEN SCHWARTZ

CELLO

DANCING THROUGH LIFE

Words and Music by
STEPHEN SCHWARTZ

CELLO

DEFYING GRAVITY

CELLO

Words and Music by
STEPHEN SCHWARTZ

Freely, with quiet intensity

FOR GOOD

CELLO

Words and Music by
STEPHEN SCHWARTZ

I COULDN'T BE HAPPIER

CELLO

Words and Music by
STEPHEN SCHWARTZ

I'M NOT THAT GIRL

CELLO

Words and Music by
STEPHEN SCHWARTZ

NO GOOD DEED

CELLO

Words and Music by
STEPHEN SCHWARTZ

ONE SHORT DAY

CELLO

Music and Lyrics by
STEPHEN SCHWARTZ

Copyright © 2003 Greydog Music
All Rights Reserved   Used by Permission

POPULAR

CELLO

Words and Music by
STEPHEN SCHWARTZ

WHAT IS THIS FEELING?

Words and Music by
STEPHEN SCHWARTZ

CELLO

THE WIZARD AND I

CELLO

Words and Music by
STEPHEN SCHWARTZ

WONDERFUL

CELLO

Music and Lyrics by
STEPHEN SCHWARTZ

Moderate Ragtime

A little slower

NO ONE MOURNS THE WICKED

CELLO

Words and Music by
STEPHEN SCHWARTZ